MW01195995

#SUCCESS
How Teens Can Create
Their Own Brilliant Future

Emma Aaron

10-10-10
Publishing

my title

#SUCCESS: How Teens Can Create Their Own Brilliant Future
Aaron, Emma
Published by: 10-10-10 Publishing Markham, Ontario
Copyright © 2016, 2017, 2019 by Emma Aaron

2024

First 10-10-10 Publishing paperback edition July 2016
Second 10-10-10 Publishing paperback edition July 2016
Third 10-10-10 Publishing paperback edition July 2017
Fourth 10-10-10 Publishing paperback edition March 2019

ISBN: 978-1-77277-083-4
- provided by publsdy

medical disclaimer

Contents

*I dedicate this book to every teenager
who is opening it with curiosity,
open-mindedness, and enthusiasm.
And, of course, I dedicate this book to Mr. Hubbard.*

either personar
persmad reason

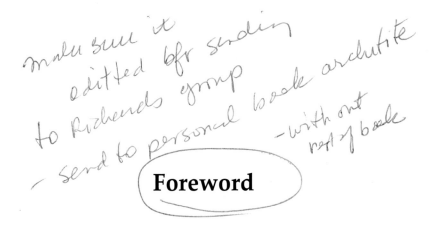

Foreword

Dear Reader ...

Do your parents complain about your behaviour, grades in school, habits, attitude, language, or friends? Do your parents praise you for what a wonderful adult you are growing into?

Are you healthy and athletically gifted, or, are you more intellectually inclined? Are you musical? Do you love reading?

No matter what your current estimation is of yourself, you are, nevertheless, a wonderful young person intent on doing something wonderful in your life.

As I'm sure you know, being a teenager is sometimes hard, and can be very confusing. But, if you are interested in learning how to succeed or build on the success that you have already achieved, then you have found the right book! Emma will teach you everything you need to know.

Ever since I was a little girl, I always knew that I wanted to be an actress. How did I do it? Well, it took much more than simply talent. I have learned that hard work and discipline are indispensable qualities when it comes to achieving your dreams. Indeed, I did the very things that Emma discusses in this book.

Emma intends to help you rise from wherever you are at the present moment to whatever greatness you desire. Have fun!

Erika Tham, Teen Actress

Acknowledgements

I would first like to thank my dad, **Raymond Aaron,** for guiding me in the process of writing this book and for encouraging me every step of the way. It is because of his wisdom and energy that I was able to get my book done so quickly. He really is the best coach and the best dad. I have learned so much from him and I am lucky to be his daughter.

I would like to thank my mom, **Lisa Janssen,** for raising me to be the person that I am today. I would not have been able to achieve all of my success if not for the endless love, admiration, guidance, and patience that she gives me. From watching my mom, I have learned the immense value of helping others.

Thank you to **Karyn Mullen,** as well, for supporting me and treating me like her own daughter. I admire how quickly and effortlessly she is able to achieve her goals and I have learned so much about how to create the things that I want in my life. She is one of the funniest people that I have ever met, and also the most caring.

I appreciate everything that I have learned from my **Aunt Susan** about spontaneity, joy, and healing. Not only has she helped people all around the world become more emotionally free, but she has also recently become an extraordinary painter and has had her work featured in multiple art shows. She is a wonderful teacher and has helped me to develop my own artistic abilities.

I am extremely grateful to one of the most amazing people in the whole word, **Meir Ezra,** for his life-changing seminars and unparalleled ability to help others. I am honoured to be able to call him my mentor and friend.

I deeply appreciate the wisdom of **Dr. Nido Qubein,** whose coaching I have received indirectly through my dad and Karyn. His insights have helped me to view situations more clearly and find opportunities to create WOW experiences in my life.

I would like to thank my English teacher, **Ms. Neff,** for instilling in me a love of language and literature. The three years of guidance she gave me has made an invaluable impact on the person that I have become.

I would also like to thank my music teacher, **Mr. Marlés.** It is because of him, that I was able to recognize my love for music and make so much progress with my flute. I deeply appreciate the many hours that he spent with me in after-school tutorials and how he has given me opportunities to perform solos in front of large audiences. I admire his extensive knowledge of music and I have been greatly inspired by him.

Of course, I would like to acknowledge all of my friends for being such amazing people and for inspiring me every day. They encourage me to take risks, learn new things, and be the best person that I can be. My friends are truly remarkable people and I am so lucky to have each and every one of them in my life.

I would like to acknowledge **Bobbi DePorter,** founder of SuperCamp®, for her amazing work with teenagers. I attended SuperCamp® and it truly was a transformational experience for me. I didn't think it was possible to have so much fun while learning! That week at camp really inspired me to conquer my fears, be more open-minded, and to live in the moment.

Last but not least, I extend a huge thank you to **Martin Rutte.** He once wrote to me, "My heart and soul and spirit always jump for joy when I hear from you," and I feel the same way about him. I'm so grateful for everything that he has taught me about business, and I admire how powerfully he is creating Heaven on Earth. Thanks, Uncle Martin. :)

1
The End

Hello and welcome to my book!

WHY DOES IT START AT "THE END?"

I hope you noticed the name of this chapter and that you are currently scratching your chin and furrowing your brow, while pondering the deep metaphorical meaning behind it.
Let me explain.

I want to start this book by explaining what the end will look like. My purpose here is to share some tips for success and give you a different viewpoint that you can use to consider the situations in your life right now. By the end of this book, I hope to instill in you a renewed confidence and joy for life.

Most importantly, I want you to decide what your own purpose is for reading this; it can be anything at all, as long as it is true for you. Use this purpose to guide you through the material that you read and the topics that you choose to implement. You may choose to read this book for some tips to help you improve your grades, study faster, improve your relationship with your parents, or anything else that is relevant to your life at the moment.

If someone is forcing you to read this book, then I have some good news for you ... it is a really good book, and that person has impeccable taste!

If you are reading it because of natural interest to thrive and be successful, then congratulations, you've come to the right place! Regardless of how this book came to be in your possession, I am so happy that you are here and are willing to learn the tips that I will be sharing.

WHAT WILL CHANGE?

Some of the things that I will be teaching are:

- How to create and maintain close relationships
- How to stick to your integrity and have confidence
- How to study faster
- And much, much more!

If you read right to the end of the book, I guarantee that you will gain many insights and will be motivated to immediately apply what you learn. And, the faster you implement these tips into your life, the better the results will be.

W.I.N.S.

To help you keep track of what you are learning, I have provided a full page at the end of each chapter with the acronym W.I.N.S written across the top. It is an acronym that I created, that stands for What I Now See. On these pages, you can write your biggest insights or realizations, you can copy down your favourite points from the chapter, or you can set goals for yourself, etc. It is simply a page at the end of every chapter that is dedicated to helping you organize your thoughts and record them so that you don't forget.

DEFINITION OF "SUCCESS"

Success, success, success. You probably hear this word all the time from your parents or teachers. You hear that you must do this and that in order to be successful or that you won't get anywhere in life if you are not successful. Do you want to be successful? Of course, we all do. So, it should be easy for you to give me the definition of the word success, right? If I asked 10 different people what success means, I would expect to get 10 different answers, and most of them would probably be examples instead of actual definitions.

How can we all be using the word "success" if we don't have an understanding of what the word actually means? To clear up this issue, the definition of the word success that I will be using throughout this book is: The sum of all validated improvements.

If you look at this definition closely, you will have a few major insights. First of all, the fact that it is a 'sum' means that the improvements build off of each other. When you acknowledge yourself once, it does not go away; it adds onto the other times that you have acknowledged yourself. It makes a big impact.

Secondly, it does not matter how big the improvement is. It is not the size of the improvement, but rather the plentifulness with which you acknowledge those improvements that is important. Keep in mind that when you have any kind of improvement, it counts for nothing if it is not validated by anyone (including yourself).

It is important that you notice your improvements for yourself and validate them. Recognize and affirm the value of every improvement that you have in all areas of your life.

When you have an improvement, validate it, when you have another improvement, validate it, and so on and so forth, and pretty soon your success will skyrocket!

Here is an example: if you are learning how to play a new instrument, then maybe on the first day you learn three notes, and then the next day you learn another three notes, and the day after that you can play a simple song, and a week after that you can move your fingers with more confidence and dexterity.

There are two things that can happen here:

1) You choose to have the mindset where you validate every improvement and continue to have more and more success.

2) You ignore all of the improvements and eventually decide that you will never be able to play this instrument.

By knowing the definition of success here, you can see that you would continue to make considerable progress and be able to play that instrument with proficiency in no time.

On the other hand, failing to validate yourself would lead to no success or very, very slow and arduous progress.

By learning the definition of the word "success," you now know the first key to achieving it — validate every improvement you make, no matter how small, and find ways to validate the improvements of other people around you!

SETTING A GOOD EXAMPLE

It is extremely important to set a good example for others. As you go through this book, you will learn things that you will apply to your life, and this will change the way that you think and the things that you do. Simply by applying all of these concepts yourself, you will have an amazing impact on the people around you.

Instead of having to teach all of these lessons to everyone that you know, simply improving yourself and implementing the tips that I will share with you, can improve the lives of the people around you. There is some pretty awesome stuff here, and it has the potential to really help you and the people you know and care about. If you want to be seen as a leader, a role model, an advisor, or a mentor, then remember to constantly be setting a good example.

The idea of success alone is a great thing to begin implementing. The next time you notice someone make an improvement, genuinely acknowledge him/her and make sure that the communication is received.

Consistently acknowledging people who have made improvements means that they will become more successful. Once they see the value of acknowledgements, they will begin to acknowledge other people in their lives. Therefore, you can see that helping one person has an affect on you and on people that you may not even know.

Let's say you have roommates who make their bed every morning. You will notice their beds are made every day and will feel bad about the fact that yours isn't made. Even if they do not ask you to make your bed, eventually you will want to because you realize that you want to measure up to that higher standard. It would be inspiring to see someone making an effort to keep a clean and orderly space. As you will learn in the next chapter, we tend to do things that we see other people doing.

AN EXAMPLE FROM MY OWN LIFE

I have attended a very difficult private school for the past 13 years. As I got older, the classes became progressively harder and by the time I got to grade eight, my entire life was consumed by school and homework. I was going to bed at 1 a.m. every night because I had so much homework to do. I was getting good marks, but I was really struggling with how to get my homework done faster, while still maintaining the same quality of work. I felt completely swamped with homework all the time and it became overwhelming. I knew that it was ridiculous for me to have this problem in grade eight, yet I could see no way out of it.

But then, I became friends with a girl in my grade who was able to get all of her homework done by 7 p.m. be asleep by 9 p.m., and still get almost the same marks as me! We were achieving almost the same results, but with very different methods. I knew that there was a lot I could learn from her.

As I got to know her better, I realized her approach to schoolwork was completely different from mine, and because of that, she was able to get her homework done much faster. By learning from her, I realized that I could have control over my homework and study schedule and I could handle everything easily without ever feeling overwhelmed. I realized that my biggest barrier before was simply my viewpoint. As soon as I got home, I would often dread opening my laptop and textbooks and confronting the daunting homework assignments that I had been given. Once I learned to change my viewpoint, I was able to look for the most efficient ways to get my work done and eliminate the distractions that had been adding extra time. When I approached my work with this causative attitude, I suddenly felt like I could have control over it, instead of letting the work control me.

Just by being friends with her, my whole viewpoint of school was broadened; I became so much more productive simply because I had a role model who taught me that it was possible.

Simply by watching someone else who could do something that I couldn't, I was able to make a big change in my life. That's the power of setting a good example. You never know what kind of effect you will have on someone just by being the best person that you can be. People may look up to you without you even realizing, it because of something special that they see in you. With this knowledge, you have a responsibility to use it to improve not only your own life, but also the lives of others.

W.I.N.S. & THE NEXT CHAPTER

Record your W.I.N.S. on the following page. Once again, this can be your insights, goals, or favourite topics from this chapter. Feel free to write down whatever you want.

Now that you know why it is important to set good examples for others, you are ready to read the next chapter, which discusses the qualities of a role model.

Emma Aaron

W.I.N.S.

2
Island of Individuality

You must take a stand to be different - you must be unique.

Embrace the things that set you apart from others, because successful people did not become successful by being the same as everyone else. The majority of people actually are not successful, so why do the things that they are doing?

Find ways to be different and don't worry about getting bullied or teased for your differences. In fact, the only people who can be affected by bullying are people who agree, or let themselves agree, with what the bullies are saying. For example, if someone told you that your left hand is too big, it probably wouldn't bother you at all because you've never thought that your left hand is too big. However, if you think that you have ugly ears, it would be easy for someone to tease you about them. This all stems from your viewpoint, not an actual fact.

An example is that if a woman in the U.S. did not shave her legs, people might laugh and make jokes about it; the consideration here is that women should not have hair on their legs. Now, move this same woman to France and you will see that hardly anyone would care. The woman didn't change; the only difference was the considerations that people had. This woman might feel more comfortable in France, but the truth is that if she maintained the same confidence in her appearance, regardless of what other people thought, she would feel comfortable anywhere.

If you totally own your differences, either those with which you were born, or those you create yourself, then you will be untouchable. Nothing that anyone says can bother you if you know what is true about yourself.

Think about it — every single person is unique and has differences, yet there are certain people who get bullied for their differences. Why? Some people feel threatened by competent people and try to attack them and lower their self-confidence. However cheesy this may sound, it can only have an affect on you if you let it.

Bullies have insecurities and therefore feel that they need to bring you down. If a bully sees you showing a spark of passion, motivation or potential, that bully will try to squish it to bring you down to their low level. But, if you totally own the things that make you different, then nothing that they do can affect you because you will be on a much higher level than them.

The best way to be invisible and unnoticed is to do the same things as everyone else. But, you won't create greatness in your life that way. Like I said at the beginning of the chapter, no one became successful by being just like everyone else. Be strong. Stand out. Go for it. Be different, and be proud of your differences. The other option, of being quiet and invisible, is a sad way to go through life.

If you face a problem with bullying, decide to give them no meaning. Give them no attention. Give them none of your energy. Put them on a useless shelf and go on with your life.

WAYS TO BE DIFFERENT

Some good ways to be different are:

- having good marks
- focusing on aesthetics
- giving speeches
- being a top athlete
- inviting students who sit alone to join you for lunch
- always voicing your opinions

Some bad ways to stand out would be:

- doing drugs
- skipping school

- breaking rules
- fighting with people
- not handing in assignments
- speaking badly to parents, teachers, or fellow students

The reason why this is important is because you are plotting your own course right now. If you choose to work on good habits as a teen, those are the habits you will have as an adult. Be a punctual teenager, then you will be a punctual adult. Do drugs as a child, and you could end up addicted as an adult. Do the things now that will get you closer to your goals in life.

If you try to be the same as everyone else, you will be invisible. You will drown in the Sea of Sameness.

If you stand out in a positive way, then you will be standing tall and proud on the Island of Individuality. There, now the title of this chapter makes sense :)

There are certain differences I have that I had no control over – like having red hair or a last name that starts with two A's (which puts me at the top of every list!).

And, then there are ways that I choose to stand out — like always participating in class discussions, asking lots of questions, befriending kids that don't have many friends, learning 210 digits of Pi, doing academic competitions, and performing my flute at concerts and assemblies. Because of that, almost everyone at my school knows my name and who I am.

DUBAI

A family moved to Canada from Dubai and they were interested in sending their kids to my school, so they scheduled a tour. Out of all of the students in the school, my best friend and I were selected to guide the tour! We were given the responsibility of showing one of the kids around the school and bringing her to all of our classes.

So what that I was chosen to guide a small tour at my school?

It is true that that incident is not a big deal, but it shows the path that I am on. The student who gets selected by the principal now is likely the one who will continue to stand out as an adult. The student who stays under the radar or is always in trouble is plotting a course towards a monotonous or trouble-making future. The first kind of student gains respect and authority – the other two do not.

CHALLENGE THE STANDARDS

Everybody that is super famous and is well-known all around the world, got there because they disagreed with previous axioms and chose not to be the same as everyone else. They did things that challenged what was possible. They challenged previous standards, and challenged people's concept of what was socially acceptable.

For example, no one says: "Wow, Bob is great. He wakes up every morning and gets to work at 9 a.m., works eight hours a day, comes home, has a beer over dinner, goes to sleep, then does the same thing the next day. When he turns 65, he will retire, move to Florida and live the rest of his life there unhappily with his second or third wife." No one says that because it is not interesting or inspiriting. It is totally in the Sea of Sameness.

There's nothing special or exceptional about that guy named Bob.

But, people do say: "Wow, Steve Jobs created the Apple computer, which has turned into a whole Apple empire. He made such a huge impact on millions of people around the world. He created something that was never thought of before."

People do say: "Wow, Malala is fighting for women's rights. She values education and knows that it should be as accessible to women as it is to men."

Only the people who are willing to take a stand and challenge what is possible are the people who really make it. If you are not willing to stand out and be different, then you are the same as everyone else and will not have an extraordinary reputation.

I'm not trying to tell you that you have to become famous in order to be successful. Success is different from person to person and does not have to be determined by income or popularity – it is whatever you decide. What I am trying to say is that the way to get there involves challenging standards and being different. You now have the second key of success.

W.I.N.S. & THE NEXT CHAPTER

As always, it is important to put into your own words what you have learned in this chapter. What cognitions? What realizations? What actions are you now contemplating? Go to the W.I.N.S. page following this page and record whatever is significant to you. Reading this book is nowhere near as important as applying what you learn.

Now that you know the importance of being different from others, read the next chapter to discover why teenagers actually have a secret advantage over adults!

W.I.N.S.

3
Teens > Adults!

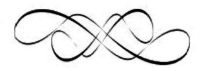

Teens have such a huge advantage over adults because we have more energy, creativity, boldness, imagination, passion and determination than they do.

USE WHAT YOU'VE GOT

So use it! If you are willing to do big things now, then for the rest of your life you will be able to say that you became successful as a teenager.

Typical adults are slower and less imaginative than children simply because they've learned to become more serious through all of the years that they've been beaten down by life.

Adults have had to change into a more professional and "adult" personality.

When adults make a big impact in the world, it is expected because they do it all the time. They are the ones that are supposed to be making the big impacts! People like Steve Jobs, Oprah Winfrey, and Ellen DeGeneres are famous, but they are adults so it is not as attention grabbing.

But, when a teenager makes a huge impact, such as Malala, it is a huge deal. Some people think that children are not as important as adults because we supposedly are not as mature or intelligent. However, the reality is that children are the same as adults, just in smaller bodies. We have the same emotions, desires, and necessities as adults. If anything, the only real difference is that we have more creativity, imagination, and determination.

BE FRIENDS WITH ADULTS

The adults that you probably spend the most time with are your parents/guardians and your teachers, and I believe that those people should be treated like friends. Teachers have dedicated their whole lives to helping children. Even if you don't think they are doing a very good job, which they sometimes are not, it is still a very noble thing that they have done, and with great intentions.

Admire your parents and your teachers and see what happens. Treat them the same way that you treat your friends that are your own age. What I mean by this is that you should give them your admiration, give them your trust, give them your patience – and you will see that your relationships with adults will become much stronger.

Keep in mind these are real, not fake, relationships. We're probably all familiar with some "teachers' pets." I truly admire my teachers for their dedication and commitment to helping kids shape their futures. I'm always willing to stay after class and talk to my teachers, do extra work for them, or give them my feedback on anything. Teachers are generally interested in helping their students succeed, so they value the information that you share with them.

THE COMFORT ZONE

In the last chapter we talked about the benefits of being different and standing out. But understand that to be different can require a lot of bravery. If you have always tried to blend in and go along with what everyone else was doing, then this will be a startling change for you. In this chapter, you will uncover the secrets of stepping out of your comfort zone.

You feel comfortable in your comfort zone because it includes only the things that you've done before, can easily experience, and are easily willing to accept. The reason why this is a bad thing is because it inhibits you from doing anything new. If you are happy to just stay in the same cycle and do the same things as everyone else, then like I already discussed, you will be in the Sea of Sameness.

You might be quite willing to stay within your comfort zone, but that is a very unadventurous way to live. A ship is safest in the harbour, but that is not what ships are built for.

Trying new things, being spontaneous and daring, and facing fears are ways to get out of your comfort zone. Doing something thrilling, such as zip-lining, skydiving, or going on a huge roller coaster, will break you out of your comfort zone because those are things that involve more motion than you are used to in your everyday life.

Now, I do not mean that you should dedicate your life to scary roller coasters. I mean only that doing what is outside your comfort zone builds your bravery so that you can take on meaningful challenges in your life. Stepping out of your comfort zone can include little changes to your life such as saying hello to more people, wearing different kinds of outfits, taking on new projects, or joining a new club. Consider doing things that will break you out of a monotonous routine or challenge a fixed idea that you have.

Examples of what I have done to get myself out of my comfort zone:

- I went indoor skydiving with my dad
- I went on vacation to the North Pole

- I am going to a boarding school in another country, three time zones away from my parents
- I wanted to improve my speed at running a mile, so I started going out to practice by myself (which was totally new to me!)
- My music teacher gave me one day's notice to play a brand new piece of music on my flute at an assembly at another school, and I did it!
- I entered a science competition against students who were 2 years older than me.
- I went zip-lining in Costa Rica and Hawaii
- I ride Canada's tallest and faster roller coasters

These are examples of more extreme things that happen every once in a while, but there are opportunities available every day to take a step out of your comfort zone. You do not have to wait until the next time you go to an amusement park or break a personal record to experiment with this – find ways to make changes in your life now!

You will find that being open to opportunities around you and doing scary, out-of-the-comfort-zone things, usually turn out to be the proudest moments of your life. Now, when confronted with a scary opportunity, I am easily able to accept it. Even if it scares me, I know the benefits of taking every opportunity that allows me to be outside of my comfort zone.

The only time you ever feel exhilarated or really alive is when you are out of your comfort zone. This makes perfect sense, because those feelings cannot exist within the realm of everything that you've experienced before. They can only exist when you are trying things for the first time, or confronting something that is scary for you. Living outside of your comfort zone is the best place to be. It is the only place you can truly be on the Island of Individuality because living outside of your comfort zone means that you are willing to experience new and thrilling things for the first time. That alone can, and will, set you apart from everyone else.

STARTING YOUNG

If you think of the average person, they lead rather uneventful lives. But, if you are willing to do whatever fun and adventurous thing presents itself, then you can be different from everyone else.

And, like I already said, teenagers have the advantage over adults because we have so much more energy, creativity and motivation, so you can easily distinguish yourself from other people just by doing things that should already be easy for you because of your young age and open-mindedness.

There are so many advantages to starting your successes at an early age. The first, and probably the most important, is that if you start young you have the rest of your life to build off of it. Changing the world when you are 90 years old is not the most ideal time, because there isn't much time left to grow. But, when you make a difference in your teen years, then there's so much potential for expanding it throughout your lifetime.

Also, kids have the power to do so much more than adults because most adults have been beaten down by life. They've experienced failures, divorces, embarrassments, rejections, illnesses, disappoint-ments, mistakes – and the emotional scars that those leave limit what they are willing to do thereafter.

When you've had so many failures, at a certain point you want to stop trying. But, children haven't experienced those things. Children are willing to say, "you be a mermaid and I'll be the shark." "Let's pretend that we're astronauts." "Oh no! The floor is covered in molten lava!" Kids are willing to use their imagination to the fullest potential and are not worried about making mistakes.

Also, as a teen, you don't have the extra responsibility of having to produce income, pay a mortgage, pay income taxes, etc. All this makes most adults very serious and solemn about life. They sometimes give up on their dreams in order to have a stable salaried job where they know that they will be getting a pay check every week, as well as benefits and vacation days. To most people, that seems like a much better option than venturing out into the unknown and having an undetermined, uncertain future.

Teenagers are more qualified, can make a larger impact, and don't have any of the barriers that adults have. I hope you are starting to see how much better it is to make an impact now, as a teen. There are so many possibilities.

W.I.N.S. & THE NEXT CHAPTER

As always, it is important to put into your own words, what you have learned in this chapter. What cognitions? What realizations? What desires? What actions are you now contemplating? Go to the W.I.N.S. page following this page and record whatever is significant to you. Reading this book is nowhere near as important to you ultimately as what you record on the W.I.N.S page. Remember, it stands for What I Now See.

Right now, think of three things that you could do that are a bit weird or tough, or scary or uncomfortable for you. Then, figure out a way to do at least one of them.

It will definitely change your life.

And, now that you've realized in this chapter that it is way better to use what you've got, befriend adults, get out of your comfort zone, and start young – you are totally ready to create any life that you want for yourself, which will be covered in the very next chapter.

W.I.N.S.

_____

_____

_____

_____

_____

_____

_____

_____

_____

_____

_____

_____

_____

_____

_____

_____

_____

_____

_____

_____

4
Purple Isn't Green

In this chapter you will learn how to make reading more enjoyable - even if it is from a textbook! And, it does not matter if you are already an avid reader or if you have never read a book in your life. I know you may devour books and absolutely love reading, or you would rather do ANYTHING besides reading. But, no matter who you are, or where you sit on that scale, this chapter will help you! So let's get started.

MAJOR REASON FOR NOT READING AND NOT ENJOYING READING

I hear all the time that the reason why people don't like reading, especially non-fiction books, is that it makes them really tired, so they want to stop reading. Sometimes they even fall asleep while studying for a test because of this sudden wave of tiredness. If you don't understand what you are reading, then of course you are going to feel frustrated and want to stop.

Being tired when reading is a manifestation of not knowing the definition of the words that you are reading. This is why people tend to feel tired when reading a complicated textbook, but would never feel tired reading a children's picture book. If you come across a word that you are unfamiliar with, it is imperative that you look it up.

Again, imagine that you are reading that children's book. It has big pictures, a big font, and easy words. You can read that with no problem; you read that without getting frustrated or confused. The only difference between reading that and a textbook is that in a textbook there are lots of words that you don't understand, crammed together in a small font.

Once you start defining those words and are able to use them properly, you will have no trouble reading. If you currently dislike reading, this will help you to overcome your objections to reading. And, if you already love reading, this will help you improve your speed and comprehension. Without looking up words, you will retain only a small percentage of what you have read.

Teachers sometimes say, to understand words you need context. This is completely wrong. How are you supposed to know the definition of a word by reading words that are beside it? If an entire class of students were given a page to read containing unfamiliar words that they had to understand based on 'context,' every single student would end up with a different idea of what those words mean and therefore none of them would actually understand what they had read. Understanding a word by context is synonymous with using your imagination to create a definition that is likely wrong or incomplete.

Read the following sentence: Mom looked up and said to her son that the doctor was going to take a look at his hallux to find the cause of the pain.

I am sure you do not have any idea what hallux means. Even worse, you may have created an instant picture in your mind of what is wrong with that child. What was your idea? Was there something wrong with the child's heart, lungs, eyesight, kneecaps, nose??? If the book went on to talk about the solutions, you'd be lost because you'd have no picture, no idea of what this thing "hallux" is.

So, there's your first homework of this chapter. Look up that word.

Your second item of homework is to think of every word in this book that you have already read and skimmed by, hoping for the best. Find them. Look them up. Understand them. Notice how your enjoyment of my book is improving!!

The urge to fall asleep because you do not know the meaning of a word is so powerful that people usually read at night to put themselves to sleep. When you read a book at night, without a dictionary or device beside your bed, you may come across a word that you do not understand, which will definitely make you feel tired.

It is very important to look up words because, if you don't, you won't understand what you are reading, and you will not want to read anymore.

Ideas are communicated through words and symbols; therefore by understanding all of the words and symbols within the topic, you will understand that topic. If you are studying for a test, all you have to do is make sure that you have no misunderstood words in that topic and you will be good to go. This will make studying fun and fast. Guaranteed.

Think of something that you know a lot about. Maybe sports. Now think of explaining that topic to somebody else. The only reason why it would be hard for them to understand is if they do not know the advanced terminology that you are familiar with. I hope it is starting to make more sense now.

Just by completely understanding every word within the topic, you will understand that topic perfectly. This reduces the amount of time it takes to study for a test dramatically, and it also improves your chances of getting a higher mark.

CHARTREUSE

So now let me tell you a funny story. My dad and I were talking one day and the word "chartreuse" came up. We were discussing the colour of something and he was trying to sound fancy, so he used that word and proudly explained to me that it meant purple. He also said that it was his absolutely favourite word and he loved whenever he had a chance to use it. The word "purple" is so ordinary, so he jumps at the chance to use the fancier word "chartreuse."

We looked it up. To my dad's astonishment and horror, it actually means "pale greenish yellow." There we go; now the title of this chapter makes sense. So, now you can see that when you are reading and you don't know a word and go past it, two problematic things will happen. One, you are missing out on that idea. But, even worse, if there is a word that you assume you know the definition of and keep going then you actually have a totally incorrect understanding of what is happening. And, of course, you are falling asleep.

W.I.N.S. & THE NEXT CHAPTER

What I Now See is, of course, next. What have you used or noticed or learned in this chapter? What decisions have you made for yourself and your life? What changes will you immediately make? Record those important ideas on the W.I.N.S. page while they are fresh in your mind.

Now that you know how fatal it is to go past a word you do not understand, and how enjoyable reading can be with understood words, the next lesson becomes even more valuable – it is all about determination and perseverance. And, it is coming up in the very next chapter.

W.I.N.S.

_____

_____

_____

_____

_____

_____

_____

_____

_____

_____

_____

_____

_____

_____

_____

_____

_____

_____

_____

_____

_____

_____

_____

5
Tacos?

You can create whatever you want in life. I know that may sound hard to believe because everything around you is trying to convince you otherwise.

DEFINITION

Based on what you learned in the chapter on misunderstood words, I am sure you know that I am now requiring you to look up the word 'create.' Look it up. Learn its meaning. Use it in a few sentences. Become friends with that word.

THEY WILL TRY TO STOP YOU

Do you remember, at the beginning of the book, when I explained that bullies have to stomp on any spark of motivation, inspiration or power that they see in you because they are trying to stop you from having success? That kind of suppression has likely happened to you, and after a while, you decide that maybe they are right. You stop thinking of yourself as super able and super powerful, capable of creating anything. You begin to believe them.

If someone tries to tell you that you cannot do something, it is because they know that you can. The proof is that no one would walk up to a wall and inform the wall that it can't talk. No one states obvious things like that. If there was something that you actually couldn't do, no one would bother mentioning it. But, as soon as someone knows that you can do something, that's when they will try to tell you that you can't.

The truth is: you can do whatever you want, and create whatever you want. Just go out and do it. Remember the chapter on doing things outside your comfort zone. Here is your chance.

If you want to have more friends, go up and talk to more people at school. If you want to become a leader, then join the student council. If you want to be more musical, join the band. If you want to dance better, take dance lessons. It actually is quite easy when you think about it. If you want to be more joyful, hang around joyful people.

An old North American Indian legend will serve well right now...

An elderly Indian chief was telling a story to an eager gathering of young boys crowded attentively at his feet. The elder explained that there are two wolves inside you. One totally supports you and urges you on to greatness. That one is powerful, strong, and wise and protective of you. "However," warned the chief menacingly, "there is an evil wolf inside you too. His job is to harm you by weakening you, by lowering your self-esteem, by inviting you to doubt yourself. Those two wolves fight constantly within you. And, quite quickly, one of them wins."

Then the old chief rose slowly and began walking away. One of the boys yelled out: "Which one wins?"

The chief stopped, slowly turned to the band of boys in rapt attention awaiting his next words. "The one you feed," he replied.

Wow, the one you feed. Do you complain with friends about how unfair life is, how bad teachers are, how unsafe the world is, and how terrible criminals are? Do you complain about your parents and the unfairness of exams? Do you hear your parents bemoan that they hit every red light on the way home? Or, that they couldn't find a parking spot? Or that it rained right after they got a car wash?

Or, do you marvel at the miracles of the universe? Do you stand in awe at the joys of life, of living, of taste, of fine art, of happiness? Is WOW a frequently used word in your vocabulary?

What you put your attention on in life is what you will receive. People who are focused on speaking badly of others, will always be aware of the faults in other people so that they have something to complain about. People who love to give praise will only notice the good in others. That is why two people can have completely different opinions about the same person. You have the power to control your viewpoint, and this determines, which "wolf" survives.

Think of the things that you want to create and you will immediately find a way to do it. Just make sure you follow through with it. Your intentions are always good, so keep that in mind whenever something goes wrong. Don't let problems bring you down. Be determined and motivated, and break through any barriers in your path. Have 100% confidence in your abilities and charge through any problem that presents itself.

TACOS

One day my mom was driving me to school and she asked me what I wanted for dinner that night. I thought for a while and told her I wanted tacos.

She said that she had to stay late at work and it would take an hour to drive home so the grocery stores would already be closed. So, she asked me what I wanted instead, and I said, "I want tacos."

She began to plan how to get someone to buy the ingredients for us and drop them off at our home. We didn't want to simply buy tacos from a restaurant because building them yourself is the fun part.

I said that everything would work itself out and that we wouldn't have to arrange anything. I told my mom to just let the subject drop and let everything handle itself.

My mom agreed to my plan but was not convinced that tacos would magically appear.

My mom got to work and immediately sent me a text that the president of the company had bought lunch for everyone — a taco lunch to be delivered to the office as a surprise. Nobody knew about it in advance. There was a lot of extra food left over, so everyone was allowed to bring some of the leftovers home for their families!!!

No matter how crazy your goal is ... Go for it! Create it! Do what it takes. You have endless possibilities and so much power.

W.I.N.S. & THE NEXT CHAPTER

As always, record your W.I.N.S. on the following page. The idea of being able to create whatever you want is totally fascinating and totally true! Think of some examples of when you thought something or wanted something, and then it actually happened. It may have seemed like a coincidence, but I'm sure you've heard the expression "There are no such things as coincidences."

Now that you know a little about creating, the next thing you need to learn is how to make studying more fun and fast. And, as always, it is in the very next chapter.

W.I.N.S.

_____

_____

_____

_____

_____

_____

_____

_____

_____

_____

_____

_____

_____

_____

_____

_____

_____

_____

_____

_____

6
Mirror-acles

MIRROR + MIRACLES = MIRROR-ACLES

What?

OK, let me explain.

This chapter will be about how to make miracles happen from mirroring other people. Hence, mirror + miracles = mirror-acles.

The people who you hang out with most are probably people who *are* very similar to you, therefore you likely *do* very similar things. Have you ever noticed that when you started hanging out with someone new you started using certain words or expressions that they use, or you might do certain actions that they do? Well, if you have successful friends, you will learn from who they are and what they do, and you will become more similar to them simply by spending more time with them. Hanging out with people who are good at things that you want to be good at, will help you understand their successful actions and gain the tools to do those things yourself.

The people you hang out with at school actually play a big role on your grades. Since you spend so much time with friends, they are the people that you emulate and get advice from; their qualities and characteristics influence you and the person that you are. Your friends have an influence on how you spend your time and the choices you make. Your grades are probably similar to those of the three friends you spend the most time with. Think about it for a second. How similar are your current grades to your closest friends' grades?

If you want to improve, simply learn from people who are already masters. It is important to always keep in mind what your own goals are, and align yourself with people who will work with you to forward those goals. Anyone who opposes your motion, or takes you off of your purpose is not a friend and is trying to block you from being successful.

POWERFUL EXAMPLES

I used to get low 80s in P.E. because it is not a subject that I particularly enjoy and, I am not the most athletically gifted individual. When I was in grade eight, I realized that I really wanted to improve my P.E. marks, so I started learning from one of my best friends, who happened to be the top athlete in our grade. What happened? My marks eventually rose up to 95%!

I figured out, from watching and being with her, new strategies, techniques, and ways to improve and when I implemented them, the results were amazing!

After learning what I had to do, of course, I still had to put in a lot of time and hard work. I'm not trying to say that by hanging out with experts, you will magically get results. But, what I am saying is that you can gain the essential knowledge from the experts so that you know exactly what it is that you have to work on and what the results will be. It is the knowledge of what you have to do, and the confidence to do it, that makes all the difference.

When you are not successful in an area, it means there's something that you don't know or that you are using false data; the same way that a calculator would give a wrong answer if you left out numbers or put in wrong numbers. Figuring out more things about that area, knowing where to direct your attention and energy will all have a great impact on your life and grades, and overall success.

Maybe you are interested in becoming better at math, so you find a friend who's very good at math and you notice the things that they do. Maybe you'll find that they take really good notes in class, or ask lots of questions. So, you start taking more detailed notes, asking lots of questions, doing your homework, etc. You will see that your understanding goes up and, therefore, your marks would go up as well.

Maybe you want to become better at reading, so you find someone you know who loves reading and you notice what they do. Then you take that knowledge and use it in your own life so that you can become successful in that area as well. This works the same way in any subject.

GETTING RID OF NEGATIVE INFLUENCES

If you are hanging out with friends who have marks in the low 70s, and your goal is to get in the 80s or 90s that does not usually go well because it is inconsistent. You hang out with other people who are similar to you. If you want to make a giant leap or a giant improvement, you need to be willing to break the status quo that you have established in your life. That does not mean that you need to give up those friends. All you have to do is define for yourself the goal you are trying to reach and realize that you will probably face opposition or speed bumps from people around you who are not at that level.

It is extremely helpful to have at least one person who you can look up to, and who can give you guidance in the area that you wish to improve in. Choose successful people to be friends with. Choose people you admire and look up to, and who you can have as your role models. If you are going into a new environment, such as a new school, try to become friends with the people you think will make the greatest positive impact on you. Of course, you can become friends with anyone you want. But, just ensure that you also surround yourself with people who will uplift you and encourage you to do the things that you love, and that you wish to improve in. If you have these kinds of role models as your friends, these are the people who will be giving you advice on your problems and influencing the way that you behave.

An important note here is that sucking up to people in order to get something from them is not the way this works. Pretending to be friendly with someone for your personal gain is called "propitiation" and is not the correct approach. Developing relationships with others is not about how much they can help you, but how much you can help them. This specific topic is continued in chapter three.

YOU MIRROR WHAT YOU SEE

My dad, Raymond Aaron, is a professional speaker who gives speeches and holds workshops all around the world. I started attending his presentations from a very young age. One day when I was about three years old at my dad's home, I gathered all of my dolls and stuffed animals together and carefully lined them up against a wall. My dad was watching this behaviour with curiosity and finally asked me what I was doing. I casually replied that I was holding a meeting. My Dad broke out laughing because I was doing what he does professionally. Would a three-year-old have done this if he/she hadn't seen someone else do it? Of course not. I was simply mirroring the behaviour that had been shown to me.

Here's an example in which I was the model of behaviour for others. My school announced that there was a Pi contest and the object was to memorize and recite the digits of Pi to the most number of decimal places. In Grade four, I recited 86 decimal places and came in third place, behind two Grade six students. The next year, I was the top in the school at 150 decimal places. Then, something interesting happened. Memorizing Pi "caught on." Others followed my behaviour. In the third year of the contest, when I was in Grade six, I had memorized 210 decimal places - but I came in second place! By that year, more people were invested in the competition and the standards rose dramatically.

Another example in which I was the role model was in music class. I play the flute and I totally love it! I enjoy it so much that I practice whenever I have a chance, and I have downloaded over 100 files of sheet music from the Internet. To my surprise, I achieved 100% in music one year - and I was the only one in the whole grade that achieved a perfect score. My teacher announced my mark to my classmates and clearly explained that I come for tutorials more than any other student, I practice more than any other student, I learn new pieces just for fun whereas no other students do. What happened? My fellow classmates learned what I did and saw the results that I got — and the whole class average improved that year.

In summary, people are constantly affected by what is going on around them, which can have a positive or negative effect. You improve the world by being a role model for others. Reciprocally, others improve you by being your role model.

W.I.N.S. & THE NEXT CHAPTER

As always, record your W.I.N.S. on the page following. Mirror-acles are fascinating concepts and you'll likely want to experiment. I highly recommend it. Write down ideas of how you can create mirror-acles on your W.I.N.S. page.

Now that you know about mirror-acles, in the next chapter I will be teaching you the real secrets on how to create and maintain a relationship in which mirror-acles can happen. When you see the answer, you will be blown away!

W.I.N.S.

_____

_____

_____

_____

_____

_____

_____

_____

_____

_____

_____

_____

_____

_____

_____

_____

_____

_____

_____

_____

_____

_____

7
Play a Big Game

THE IMPORTANCE OF EXCHANGE

It is essential to know how to contribute to others if you want a mirror-acle. You cannot just follow around math nerds and expect them to do your homework for you or tutor you. You cannot demand that people help you or give you their tips for improving in a certain subject. So, it is important to know how you can give back to someone in order to create strong and ethical relationships.

For example, in the story I told you in the previous chapter about how I improved in P.E. because I had a friend who is an athlete, I helped her in areas that she was struggling as well. The way that I gave back to her was by helping her with her homework after school because she wanted to improve in certain subjects. In one year, while I was improving in P.E., she improved her academics and went from an average in the 80s to an average in the 90s, and has been able to maintain that for the past two years.

If I had simply taken the skills and knowledge that she had without also being able to contribute to her, I would have no value as a friend.

I'm sure you've had the experience where you sensed that someone was only hanging out with you in order to get something from you. And, if you have had that experience before, then you know that it is not fun, and you probably found yourself not wanting to be around that person anymore; let alone give them the thing that they were trying to get from you.

However, if you are willing to give something back that is useful to the other person and is of equal value in their mind, then you will see that the relationship will work much better. There always has to be a balance; so if you get something, you give something in exchange. You do not want to have fake relationships. Do not pretend to be friends with someone so that you can get something from them – this goes back to the word propitiation that I mentioned in the last chapter.

Care about the person that you've chosen to be your mentor and contribute to them, and then you will be able to learn what they know. The best way to guarantee a meaningful and long-lasting relationship is to ensure that you are giving to the other person and that they are giving back to you.

If you just follow around talented people and pretend to be their friend, they will not want you to be around, and you will be bothersome to them. Furthermore, taking without giving has a negative impact on you as well. Imagine trying to only breathe in for the rest of your life without exhaling – it is not possible! Have you even been in a situation where someone did something extremely generous for you and you wished you had something to give back to him or her? We have a natural instinct to maintain this balance, and leaning too far to one extreme can be very damaging to relationships. If you create relationships where you do not give back to others, you will eventually not have relationships.

If you are willing to be in exchange with others for help that they give you, not only will they not mind helping you. But, they will actually go out of their way to spend more time with you so that you can benefit from each other. You'll be able to get so much more benefit if you have this kind of symbiotic relationship.

BRAIDING

Before school, at lunch, after school, and basically whenever we had free time, I would braid my friends' hair and I really enjoyed it because I saw how happy it made them.

People would come up to me with different ideas of how they wanted their hair to be styled, and then I would create the hairstyle that they asked for.

After a while, people started to recognize me as THE hair braider and whenever someone was walking around with a nice hairstyle, people would say, "Wow! Emma did a great job."

I got a positive reputation of being able to do really pretty hairstyles and whenever anyone had something hair-related to discuss, they would come to me and I would share my knowledge in that area. The people that I braided hair for gave back to me by giving me advice or tips in other areas.

Think about it like going to a store and buying something. If there is something you want to buy, you can't simply take it from the shelf and walk out; you have to give money in exchange for the product. So, if there is knowledge, expertise, guidance, or anything like that that you want to gain from someone, you have to be willing to give something back in exchange.

WHAT CAN YOU EXCHANGE?

Now you may be thinking that you don't have anything of value that you can use to contribute to other people.

Trust me; not only do you have something of value, you could probably fill up a whole page of valuable ways that you can exchange with people. Do you play sports? Do you speak a second language? Are you a trustworthy friend? Are you really gifted in a subject at school? I'm sure that you are knowledgeable or talented in a whole list of ways that other people could benefit from. You can use the talents that you already have to help others – exchange is not just about money.

And, all that relates to what you have already developed from the past. Remember that on any day of the week, you can improve at something just by starting. When you put in the energy to learn or practice something, then quite quickly, you may become more competent with it than most other people.

YOUTUBE

Now let me give you one more example of how I have implemented this. I watch a lot of YouTube videos. I noticed how entertaining it was and how many teenagers spend their time watching YouTube. However, I also noticed that hours of having fun watching more and more YouTube videos would not actually get me anywhere in life. I wondered: Is there a way to enjoy YouTube videos without feeling like I'm wasting my time?

Just by asking that question, an answer arrived. I noticed that there were certain things that all successful YouTubers do, and other things that all unsuccessful YouTubers do. And, I realized that nobody else was teaching this because when I googled, it I could find nothing that explained what I had just discovered.

I decided to become a YouTube consultant to teach people how to create and maintain successful YouTube channels. I found my dad's YouTube channel and I saw that he was not following any of the rules that I had just discovered. I was not surprised when I saw that his videos did not have very many views. Ha!!

I tested my program out on my dad and these were the results:

- After seven years on his own, he had a total of 400 subscribers. That means that he was getting around five new subscribers each month.
- After just six months of my coaching he had over 1,000 subscribers. That's 100 new subscribers each month!

My dad was amazed and impressed, and so were his clients. His business colleagues started to see the success of his YouTube channel and asked who he had hired to manage it. When my dad said that it was me, people went crazy and instantly wanted to hire me because I stood out from all other YouTube coaches because I'm a teenager. YouTube is such a popular social media site among teens, so who better to teach it than a teen?

I want you to notice something from the story. Millions of kids watch YouTube videos on a regular basis, but hardly any of them observe and look for patterns; am I right? You probably watch YouTube videos just for enjoyment, to learn something new, or to fall into the black hole of viral cat videos - and that's totally fine because that's mostly why YouTube exists in the first place.

But, I decided that since I was spending so much time watching YouTube videos, I might as well learn something from it and make it a more meaningful experience. So, there's a lesson in itself; if there is something that takes up a lot of your time, or you have the chance of experiencing often, make sure to notice trends and patterns in those things. Otherwise, you will just be allowing it to happen to you, passing up valuable opportunities.

WHAT ARE YOUR SPECIAL TALENTS?

There was a time I could not play the flute, and then there was a subsequent time when I could play very well. Same with braiding. Same with getting high grades. Same with understanding why some YouTube videos are highly viewed and others are not. Same with editing videos.

I now have a long list of what I'm really good at because I just began one day with each one and pursued it until I was really good. And, you could do the same.

By continuing to do this, you will build up a huge collection of unique talents that nobody else has, and you can use these to exchange with other people. If you simply observe the unique experiences that you have, and try to learn from all of them, then you will have a huge reservoir of knowledge that people will be inspired by.

It will be so easy for you to exchange with other people because you will have so much to offer. Instead of just going through life, find things that you are interested in, pursue things that you are curious about, and turn them into things that have a value that you can use to exchange. Helping other people opens up so many opportunities for your success.

DELIVER MORE THAN IS EXPECTED

When you are giving back to someone, you have two options. You can either give them back something of equal value, like giving money for a product, or you can blow them away and give something extra that was unexpected! Personally, I prefer the latter, because if you can have a huge impact on someone, they will remember that and will feel much appreciated.

For example, if someone gives me something and I have something that I can get back to them, then without telling them in advance, I could add something extra just to give them a WOW experience. Companies that succeed in the long run, are always operating at this level — they give more than what was paid for.

This is helpful in business as well because, let's say you are a supplier of a product to a major corporation. If you consistently give them WOW experiences, then you will stand out from all of your competitors. If there is ever a question as to whether to hire you versus another supplier, the corporation will choose you every time because they know that they will get more value from you than from anyone else.

There is a very important distinction that must be made here. Giving more than what is expected does not mean giving more of the same thing. If I gave you a product that was supposed to cost $10, but instead you gave me $11, that is not a WOW experience because you are just giving a bit more of what is expected.

However, if you pay the $10 and in addition to that you post a message on social media explaining how much you love my product and would recommend it to all your friends, that is something of enormous value that I never would have expected. If you do things like this for people, without them asking for it, their opinion of you will immediately shoot up and they will want to give back to you.

Let's take another example. Let's say I am a hairdresser and you come to me to get your hair cut. If I used this rule the incorrect way and gave you more of the same thing, then all you would be getting is even shorter hair, which isn't what you wanted! But, if I provided more by giving you a coupon or a free hair accessory, then you would be leaving the salon with a great impression.

There is something in life called the law of reciprocity. Reciprocity is the practice of exchanging things with others for a mutual benefit. If you do something small for someone, you will get something small back. If you do something huge for someone, you will get something huge back. This concept is based on the ideas that you learned in the first few chapters about the power of setting a good example for others, and how people mirror the behaviour that they see.

If someone does something small for you, like holding the door, then in return it is appropriate to give a small reaction, such as saying thank you, and keep walking. If someone does something amazing for you, out of the blue, then in return, the appropriate response would be to have a big reaction and give something in return out of gratitude. If all of your actions have implications anyway, why not do huge positive actions that will have huge positive implications? Give out the things that you want to receive. This works because of the law of reciprocity.

#Success

W.I.N.S. & THE NEXT CHAPTER

You can try this right now. Think of ways that you can give WOW experiences to other people and blow them away by implementing things that you've learned from this book. In return for that, you will get huge acknowledgements and praise, and you will probably be surprised to find out what happens as a result.

You've started learning about how to make yourself stand out from other people, so in the next chapter we will be taking that even further. You'll find out the exact method to make yourself known and become an expert in whatever areas you are interested in. Keep reading to find out how to get out of the Sea of Sameness and into the Island of Individuality.

W.I.N.S.

_____

_____

_____

_____

_____

_____

_____

_____

_____

_____

_____

_____

_____

_____

_____

_____

_____

_____

_____

_____

_____

8
Get It Done!

In this chapter, you will learn how to overcome obstacles, impress your peers, teachers, and parents, and catapult yourself to higher levels than you've ever imagined. This chapter will teach you about productivity, resourcefulness, and getting maximum reactions from minimum actions.

PERSERVERANCE

Perseverance is an invaluable asset because if you have the strength to keep going until you get the results that you want, then there is literally nothing that can stand in your way. Do not let a slight breeze blow you off course. Do not let speed bumps persuade you to slow down. Once you decide to go for something, go for it with all of your might!

One of the most valuable life lessons that I learned from going to my school, was to not stop until the job is done. This is not something that was directly taught to me, but I started doing it because I realized that I felt much better with myself when I handed in work that I was proud of. This was confirmed for me when I saw that I got better marks when I did whatever it took to get the job done — no matter what. If you implement this rule, even slightly, you will find that your ability to overcome obstacles will increase dramatically, and the people around you will be stunned by your ability to get things done.

HOW TO MAKE WORK EASY

Have you ever noticed that in an emergency, things that usually seem hard become easy? Typically a door is very hard to break through. But, if there's an emergency and you need to get through that door, suddenly you will find a way to break it open. If you are working on a project and it seems very hard, as soon as you are almost out of time, the project suddenly isn't hard anymore.

The trick is to use that same increased willingness to do things, that you experience in emergency situations, and apply that to your everyday life. The way to do this is to set targets for yourself in order to break down jobs. If there is a big project that you are working on, instead of procrastinating and waiting until the last minute, make a list of all of the things that need to be done, and then create dates by which those individual tasks will be completed. That way you will have constant deadlines to meet and it will ensure that everything gets done in an appropriate time frame.

What is the biggest mistake that you make when you are writing a list of things to be done? Well, most commonly the things that we have to do are for other people. Maybe you are working on an assignment for a teacher or finishing a job for a boss... Eventually the thing that you were working on will be given to someone else to review. The biggest mistake that people make is not knowing exactly what it is needed and wanted from them when they are doing a project or task for someone. They do not know the exact results that their teacher, boss, client, etc., are expecting. Therefore, the lists that they make consist of tasks that don't get them any closer to their goal.

Whenever, I am given an assignment at school, I always make sure to take the exact instructions and use the criteria as a guideline when I am doing my work. I ask the teachers to tell me what it is that they are looking for, and then I am able to deliver on it. I can create the best essay or presentation in the world, but if it does not match any of the criteria that was being asked of me, then I can't get any recognition or marks for it.

The way to truly blow away your teachers, is to find out exactly what it is that they are looking for, and then give them back those things. When they are reading your assignments, they will have no choice but to give you a great mark, if you have delivered on every single thing that they were looking for – especially when your assignment is of a high standard.

This can apply to anything, not just school.

If you are given a chore to do at home, find out exactly what your parents are expecting. In other words, what do they want the final result to be? Giving them exactly what their ideal outcome, is will impress them beyond belief.

RESOURCEFULNESS

Find ways to play to your strengths. Let's say you are really good at science; if you are given an essay to write in English class, try and involve science as much as possible since it is an area that you are knowledgeable in. Or maybe you are really good at sports; if you have to do volunteer hours, you can volunteer as a coach for a local team. Work on developing certain talents or skills that you enjoy and then find ways to integrate those very strong areas into more aspects of your life. This is called using what you've got or being resourceful.

By now, if you have read through this whole book, you have a massive tool belt filled with things that you can use. No matter what situation you find yourself in, know that you have the tools necessary to handle it. I wish you the best of luck!

W.I.N.S.

As always, it is important to write down what you have learned in this chapter. What cognitions? What realizations? What actions are you now contemplating? Go to the W.I.N.S. page, following this page, and record whatever is significant to you. Just reading this book is nowhere near as important as actually applying what you learn.

Now that we have reached the end of our journey, I hope that you are filled with ideas and are eager to apply the concepts that you have just learned. If you have started to apply them already, that is even better! Get ready for some big changes in your life! I can't wait to hear all about your successes. If you would like to contact me directly to share any of your W.I.N.S., or ask questions, please feel free to email me at SuccessBook@Aaron.com.

W.I.N.S.

_____

_____

_____

_____

_____

_____

_____

_____

_____

_____

_____

_____

_____

_____

_____

_____

_____

_____

_____

_____

To summarize the book, I have provided a list of all of the key ideas from each chapter so that you can return to them whenever you wish.

Chapter 1

- How to create success
- The importance of setting a good example for others

Chapter 2

- Find ways to be different from other people
- How to be proud of your differences
- Good and bad ways to be different
- The benefits of being on the Island of Individuality

Chapter 3

- The advantages that teenagers have over adults
- Why you should treat adults as friends
- How to get out of your comfort zone
- The joys of living outside of your comfort zone
- Why you should start being successful at a young age

Chapter 4

- You have more power than you believe
- How to create whatever you want
- How to have a positive mindset

Chapter 5

- How to make reading more enjoyable
- Why it is important to look up words
- What happens when you go past a word you don't know the definition of
- Why context is bad!

Chapter 6

- How you are affected by the people you spend time with
- How to mirror the behaviour of successful people
- How to get rid of negative influences

Chapter 7

- The importance of contributing to people
- How to create mirror-acles
- Finding your own talents that you can use to exchange
- How to deliver more WOW experiences

Chapter 8

- How to overcome obstacles
- How to blow away teachers and parents
- How to make work easy
- How to be resourceful

- Who you are
- family
- make it relateable

About the Author

Emma Aaron lives in Toronto, Canada, but is currently attending high school in Oregon, USA.

The author is available for delivering keynote presentations to appropriate audiences. For rates and availability, please contact the author directly at: SuccessBook@aaron.com.

To order more books, search for "#SUCCESS" on Amazon.com

Finally, if you have been inspired by this book, the best thing you could ever do is pass that on and be a wonderful role model for others. The world needs more shining lights.

add offers
promo self

do not use info @

Manufactured by Amazon.ca
Acheson, AB